IT'S OK
IF YOU'RE
CLUELESS

Demetrius 2010

Much Success
to you!

from
the Moreno-Lynn
family

Also by Terry McMillan

Mama

Disappearing Acts

*Breaking Ice: An Anthology of Contemporary
African-American Fiction* (editor)

Waiting to Exhale

How Stella Got Her Groove Back

A Day Late and a Dollar Short

The Interruption of Everything

TERRY McMILLAN

IT'S OK
IF YOU'RE
CLUELESS

AND

23 More Tips
for the
College Bound

VIKING

VIKING
Published by the Penguin Group
Penguin Group (USA) Inc., 375 Hudson Street,
New York, New York 10014, U.S.A.
Penguin Group (Canada), 90 Eglinton Avenue East, Suite 700,
Toronto, Ontario, Canada M4P 2Y3 (a division of Pearson Penguin Canada Inc.)
Penguin Books Ltd, 80 Strand, London WC2R 0RL, England
Penguin Ireland, 25 St. Stephen's Green, Dublin 2, Ireland
(a division of Penguin Books Ltd)
Penguin Books Australia Ltd, 250 Camberwell Road, Camberwell,
Victoria 3124, Australia (a division of Pearson Australia Group Pty Ltd)
Penguin Books India Pvt Ltd, 11 Community Centre, Panchsheel Park,
New Delhi–110 017, India
Penguin Group (NZ), Cnr Airborne and Rosedale Roads, Albany,
Auckland 1310, New Zealand (a division of Pearson New Zealand Ltd)
Penguin Books (South Africa) (Pty) Ltd, 24 Sturdee Avenue,
Rosebank, Johannesburg 2196, South Africa

Penguin Books Ltd, Registered Offices: 80 Strand, London WC2R 0RL, England

First published in 2006 by Viking Penguin,
a member of Penguin Group (USA) Inc.

1 3 5 7 9 10 8 6 4 2

Illustrations and hand-lettering by Joel Holland

ISBN: 0-670-03298-0

Printed in Mexico
Set in Perpetua
Designed by Francesca Belanger

For the 2002 graduating class
of St. Mary's College High School,
Berkeley, California

Introduction

Back in the stone age (circa 1969) I slept through the commencement speech at my graduation. And I wasn't the only one. All we wanted was to hear our names called so we could finally toss our caps into the air and beeline it out of there, sneak and smoke a cigarette (it was cool then) and down something with any percentage of alcohol as our reward for enduring four years of educational tyranny. We were now self-ordained adults and finally free to tell our parents that as soon as we were handed our diplomas, their eighteen-year dictatorships were now over, that from now on, we were calling the shots. We would stay up and out as long as we wanted, we would go wherever we felt like because we had passed enough tests to prove our intelligence (legitimately or not) and had finally earned the right to step into the abyss we were claiming as our future. We all had plans. Big ones. Kmart, Ford Motor Company and a ring from the local diamond jeweler were at the top of the list. I was going to save the world if I remember correctly. I didn't quite know how, but I'd deal with the small details when they came up.

I remember being nudged by someone whose last name started with an *M:* "Wake up, Terry!" I didn't know exactly what the speaker had said but I knew it was the usual drone of how bright our futures were going to be, with the speaker's using him- or herself as an example of how they had achieved success. (Most of the time we didn't think that what they did for a living sounded all that interesting or like it was much fun.) After attending a number of these ceremonies, it was clear to the graduating class of '69 that many of these speakers had nothing else going on, so this was their "fifteen minutes" and we were not going to be spared the marvelously dull, cliché-laden spiel our predecessors had endured of how hard work will guarantee us success. The faces of many Timex watches glowed as we slid the sleeves up and down our rayon gowns to acknowledge that, yes, the infamous speaker was going over the allotted time limit. We all knew we were being lied to—at least I did—because hard work had not paid off in my family. No one I knew was successful. They had jobs, not careers. A real paycheck with a few dollars left over would've been nice. I already knew that life was going to be a struggle or at least a challenge, but I was looking forward to it. Anything was possible if only you could just get there, as I'd learned from watching 77 *Sunset*

Strip and *Adventures in Paradise*. The whole idea of not-knowing what I was going to do and how I was going to "end up" as a grown-up gave me a thrill. I liked the whole concept of not-knowing since up to this point just about everything else in my life had been so predictable. I thought the not-knowing was the whole point of being a grown-up.

I found out by default what rocked me and lit me up inside. Writing felt like it chose me and instead of resisting I surrendered. It is what has kept me sane. It is how I have been able to make sense out of many things I find perplexing, myself included. And it has made this journey worthwhile.

When I was asked to give the commencement speech at my son's high school graduation in 2002, I politely declined. I wanted to sit in that audience like every other parent and wait until they got to the *W*'s to watch my son march across that stage with the special honors colors on his tassel because he turned out to be much smarter than his mother, all by his own volition. And he was going to Stanford! Months later his high school called back. They hadn't been able to find anyone and asked if I would reconsider, assuring me that the speech could be as short as seven minutes but preferably ten or twelve, and that I'd still be able to sit in the audience and watch Solomon march. I asked my son would he mind and he said no, as long as I didn't say anything that would embarrass him. And I said, "Me?"

All I knew was that I did not want my speech to put anyone to sleep. I thought back to the speeches we had heard and how little insight they had given us on what it was really going to take to deal with the chaos, uncertainty and insecurities many of us didn't even know we had. I didn't want to be boring and since it was a celebratory occasion and these kids had parties they were itching to get to (one of them being at my house later), I didn't want to talk about me. I wanted to tell them the truth. But I wanted them to feel good about their fears and uncertainties, to let them know that despite their insecurities, they stood a chance of being successes. Mostly, I wanted them to know that first they had to find their own comfort level of what success meant to them, but I also wanted to have some fun and let them know that I wasn't born yesterday and that here we are today, and this little booklet is what I wished someone had told me centuries ago. It was very cool how most of these 168 graduating students as well as their parents were actually *listening*.

These tips are no panacea. They are no guarantee for anything, but what I hoped they would do is cut these kids some slack when jumping into the sea of uncertainty called life without a raft, and that they know that this is what the journey is all about; that it's OK to be scared, but just paddle, and here were a few things to watch out for while they searched and sometimes stumbled while finding their very own little patch of the world that made them light up inside.

It has worked for me.

My son actually hugged me afterward. He told me he was very proud to be my son and that I was the coolest mom he'd ever had. I have not met The Others, but he will graduate from college in June 2006, and he has stuck by this very deep comment. It continues to tickle and amaze me, watching him discover who he is. I made it very clear to him early on that I couldn't tell him who he should be because I didn't have that right nor was I clairvoyant. Even if I was, I'd keep my mouth shut. I want him to ride these waves until he can stand on his own. So far, he's doing just fine. He makes the coolest "beats" ever and there is no major at Stanford for what he loves to do. But I told him that it was OK. He does not have to prove how smart he is to anyone or to apologize for not being a scholar. This is his life and he has the freedom to make decisions as well as change his mind. That is the luxury of being young. But I told him a little secret: that holds true at fifty and sixty and seventy, too. The goal, in my estimation, is to continue to evolve and change and renew our thinking and feelings so that we do not remain static and stuck about anything. It's how I measure my own evolution and as long as what he does pleases him and one hopes will benefit others, then he will have added something sacred to the world. I still would like, however, to have a serious conver sation about those misplaced modifiers and those gerunds he insists on using at the beginning of sentences, which drives me nuts. Perhaps over dinner (hot dogs and fries) at his crib, we will sit on the sofa since there are no chairs or table and toast the brightness of both of our uncertain futures: "Would you prefer your water in Styrofoam or plastic, Mother?" But then again, maybe not.

IT'S OK
IF YOU'RE
CLUELESS

1. Sit Up Straight and Walk Tall

There's nothing worse than watching you young people sitting with your spines curved like the Hunchback of Notre Dame, or walking as if you're afraid of something. Both make you look downright slovenly and uncomfortable with your self. So sit up straight, as if there's a board behind your back. It takes some getting used to at first, but it will begin to feel good. And walk tall, as if someone's holding your head, chest and shoulders by separate strings or, more simply: walk like you're royalty (because you are). Even if you don't have much confidence, fake it. After a while you'll get so accustomed to faking it that you won't even realize when your confidence becomes real and rightfully so. At seventeen or eighteen years old,

very few of you believe that you'll ever get old—
but believe me you will—and you don't want to
end up walking like a spoon, or, when seated,
looking like one of the golden arches.

2. Learn How to Breathe

Most of us don't realize it, but in stressful situations many of us hold our breath. Right this minute, notice how few breaths you're actually taking. Or how shallow they are: they're probably coming from your chest. Most of us don't even realize we're not inhaling and exhaling with any regularity. We're too busy thinking about a million things at once instead of just one thing or trying to get somewhere and not paying full attention to where we are. When you drive, for example, notice how you hold your breath until *after* you change lanes, turn or hit the brakes. Science has proven that the more conscious breaths you take, the more relaxed you'll feel. Try this: inhale deeply through your nostrils so that all the

BREATHE

BREATHE

BREATHE

air goes down into your stomach until you look about four months pregnant! Hold it to the count of four, then slowly exhale through your mouth to the count of seven. If you do this three or four times in a row, your shoulders will drop, your heart rate will slow down and you'll realize that you actually feel relaxed! Believe it or not I learned how to do this in church! The minister had the entire congregation breathing like this with our eyes closed. I try to do this exercise twice a day for twenty minutes. Take a crack at it and you'll be amazed at what it can do for your disposition and concentration. Might come in handy in college when you're stressing over scholarly pursuits such as "Will he call?" or "I hope she'll give me some play at the party this Saturday."

3. Don't Listen to Your Parents

Of course they mean well, but you can't live out their dreams, you have to find your own. If for whatever reason they don't like the path you chose, tough nuggies. It's your turn to live your life. They already chose theirs. So, if dad always hoped you'd be a doctor (like he is) or mom always wanted you to be the first lawyer in the family but you want to make music videos or drive a race car or paint or be a makeup artist or crunch numbers—then go for it.

4. Read Anything and Everything

Most students read only what they have to. Reading can increase your interests and make you more interesting. It will expand your awareness about many things you may never be able to see or touch or experience in real life, but it can feel like you have. Reading will make you smarter. And who doesn't want to be smarter? If you don't, then consider yourself dumb. Get used to being boring. And ignorant. Reading what you don't know much about will make you more informed. Spark your imagination. Make you think. If you don't take the time to read—anything from the newspaper to *Spin* or *Playboy* or *Out* or *People* magazine—it means you're not curious about much of anything except yourself. And if that's the case, your world will shrink as you get older. The more you know, the better off you'll be. Reading can make the difference in your life's being just a stamp on a letter or the whole envelope.

5. Do Everything with Gusto

Don't half step. Whatever you choose to do, give it everything you've got or don't do it at all. A mediocre effort will get you mediocre results.

6. Let Your Insides Match Your Outsides

Let people see the real you. Learn when it's good to follow your heart and not your brain and vice versa. Take special notice of what makes you tick. Pay extraclose attention to what's screaming inside your head and heart. This stuff wants to get out so that you don't have to live a lie. Don't be afraid to live out your fantasies. Be the kind of person you imagine yourself to be. But try not to lie or cheat or hurt other people intentionally or do whatever you can get away with in order to win or get ahead because you'll only end up losing in the long run.

7. Know That the World Does Not Revolve Around You

Take other people's feelings into account. You are not the only one who has them. Two human traits that are worth practicing: compassion and empathy. Caring about someone else's misfortune and putting yourself in another person's shoes will allow you to be less judgmental and not so super-critical of others. It will enable you to be more thoughtful, instead of so self-absorbed. Learn to accept criticism from people you respect and don't worry if you discover what many of us already know: that we are not perfect and the only way to become a better human being is to try to be more humane.

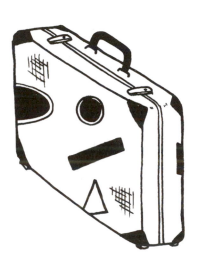

8. See the World

It is a vast and beautiful place. See as much of it as you possibly can during your lifetime. Traveling will allow you to see how other people live. It will give you a broader perspective and offer you more insight into your own way of life because you'll have something to compare it to. As corny as it may sound, seeing any part of the world will also help you appreciate the breathtaking beauty of nature and give you countless opportunities to witness firsthand the universality of all people, regardless of where they live.

9. Success Should Not Be Based on Fame or How Much Money You Make

Contrary to popular belief, you can't measure success by that SL55 in the garage, by all the labels you wear or by how big your stupid house is. All the bling bling in the world just tells people what you possess or what you think you can afford. Success is determined by the quality of your life and the amount of joy you feel on any given day. There are a lot of miserable and lonely people who are sloppy rich. The opposite often holds true as well. Ever wonder why? Feeling worthy and knowing you are doing your best and are pleased because it makes you happy is a more accurate yardstick to use. Please don't let fame and fortune be your goals. It's a trap people fall for from watching too much TV. Fame is not all it's cracked up to be and there are millions of happy and successful people who are not famous. Or rich. However, if you end up becoming famous because you earned it based on your deeds or work, not because you were striving for it, then be proud, especially if you use it in unselfish ways. Otherwise, when it fades, so will your spirit. The amount of money you make does not tell anybody what kind of person you are inside. It just tells them you have some dough. But so what? You won't be buried with any of it.

10. Life Should Be an Adventure, Not Some Predictable Experience

If at eighteen you've already figured out exactly how you plan to live your whole life, you're probably on the road to becoming a boring and unyielding person. A plan is not a bad thing but know that the quality of your life will be determined by a lot of things: mostly how you handle the unexpected detours that threaten your smooth plan and all the ups and downs that will certainly come your way. These are the biggest tests of character. It's called Life 101. It's what happens when you've planned something else. So take that belly dancing class. Make love on the beach at night. Go on and jump off the cliff and fly over the earth or dive into the royal blue sea with your eyes wide open. Kick your feet hard. Do the things that scare you. Say yes when you want to and don't worry about what people will think. They will judge you regardless, so let that be their problem. Do everything you can to make your life the most unforgettable experience ever so that by the time you're forty or seventy, you won't have a million regrets but amazing memories you might want to share with your kids one day. But then again, maybe not!

11. It's OK if You're Clueless About What to Major In

Unless you're a child prodigy or already know what intrigues you more than anything else, chances are you may not know yourself well enough to know how you want to make a living. But you don't have to know today or next week or even next year. Millions of college freshmen don't know what they want to do for the rest of their lives, and a large percentage of those who think they do end up changing their minds and their majors at least two or three times before they graduate. Molecular biology may not cut it for them after two semesters, but maybe drama class will. It's perfectly normal to be unsure of yourself, which is why you should not feel bad about changing your mind and your direction. You're only young once and not many successful folks knew at eighteen—or for some of us even at thirty—what we wanted to do with our lives. Sometimes it takes years of experimenting, failure and even disappointments before many of us discover our real interests and talents. This is the one time in your life when you can truly afford to change your mind, make mistakes and realize that the world won't come to an end when you do. So don't be embarrassed about or apologize for your uncertainty. Use your years in college to find your way, to excavate and chip away until you strike gold. You'll know when you do. So please don't settle on a major or a career because you feel pressured or think it's the right thing to do. It's your life, so treat it like it's a gift you are un-

wrapping to find out what's inside. Share the gift.
Besides, there are too many people stuck in jobs
they hate because they did this very thing. You
don't want to be one of them.

12. Make God Proud

Try to make sure there is goodness in everything you do. If we all learned to live our lives with more compassion and empathy toward others, we would never have to worry about another 9/11 or being shot in a drive-by or being betrayed by a loved one. So smile at a stranger. Look people in the eye when you talk to them. And really listen when someone is talking to you. Give somebody a compliment who doesn't expect it. Especially someone old or someone who looks like they could use one. Whatever you do, let it be something humane, something civil and civic, something honorable, even noble. What's the worst that can happen?

13. College Is a Place Where You Can Discover Who You Really Are and Get an Education at the Same Time

College is called an institution of higher learning for a reason. It is not a place where you try to impress people based on what you already know. Besides, in college no one really cares how many AP classes you've had; it's what you do while you're there that matters—not how you got there. Getting an education is an ongoing process. There are a lot of dumb people who have college degrees. The degree itself should not be your primary goal. College is where you can find out where you fit best, where you might stumble upon something that excites you. Pay attention to it—whatever it is—no matter how ridiculous it may seem. Sometimes you may not find it until years after you leave college, and sometimes there may not even be a major for it, or part of the curriculum, but do not toss it in a ditch. Oftentimes, the thing you've been doing all your life commonly referred to as a hobby is actually your calling. So pay attention to what you enjoy doing that makes you lose all sense of time and what may seem too easy. An education allows you to not just connect the dots, but to *see* the dots. Being an educated person means you are able to think discriminately, to trust your instincts and your own judgment, that you are able to see what's good and respect it, but also see what's wrong and try to fix it. Inherent with getting an education (which, by the way, is a lifelong thing) is that it makes you more curious about the world and your role in it. So don't waste your time worrying about how you're going to do in college. You'll do fine. Know that millions have come before you and made it through, and most of us weren't even close to being an Einstein or Bill Gates or Rosa Parks!

14. Homework Is History:
It's Time to Study

Believe it or not, college isn't harder than high school. Not! It simply requires that you think instead of memorize. It is where you have an opportunity to question information rather than merely apply it. Studying isn't quite up there with hard labor but it requires your sustained and undivided attention. This means not listening to 50 Cent or Beck or Nickelback or Gretchen Wilson or Keyshia Cole blasting in your iPod earphones while you're reading about the Oedipus complex or abnormal cell growth. And speaking of which, if you can't stand the withdrawal pains of the following appendages many of you seem unable to function without for more than five minutes, get over it. Turn off your cell phone, don't check your text messages, message boards, e-mail or surf the Net just because the spirit moves you. Drop out of reach and cyberspace until you handle your business. As an FYI, you might be shocked to learn that you don't really get homework in college (except maybe in math and foreign languages) and there's no such thing as extra credit and very few multiple-choice questions and rarely are you ever given a pop quiz. You will be told when you're going to be given a quiz or a test. You might also discover something else: that learning new things, gaining insight and acquiring knowledge isn't all that frightening, it's actually quite liberating, and you might even like it when you realize you have thoughts and ideas that are contrary to what you're learning. This is how you become a thinking grown-up. This is how some people have changed the world.

15. Party Hard, Work Hard

There will *always* be a party on any given college campus on any given night. But. You have to learn to parent yourself and know when to hang and when to take a rain check, even if everybody you know is going. Turn your papers in on time. Read those seventy-five pages before you go to that co-ed pajama party or to see *Scary Movie 18* or to spend most of the night with Cecil or Tiffany. Learn how to say no to your friends and to yourself. Cramming is not fun. Writing a fifteen-page paper the night before usually does not allow you to do your best work. Half the time you won't even remember writing it. So, try to look at partying as a reward, and not your right. Especially if mom and dad are footing the bill for any part of your college experience, like tuition!

16. Bring Your Dirty Laundry Home

Whenever possible. But first, offer to help do something useful around the crib before you unpack. Leave your ugly luggage or duffel bags in a high-traffic area. Your mother will notice the smell that you don't. She will offer to wash them but insist that she not waste her time. She does enough. And while you are cleaning the garage she will be unable to resist. Of course, prior to stuffing all those dingy T-shirts, mildewed towels and holey socks, bras with no elastic left in the straps and thongs (none of which may belong to you) into your laundry bag, you should have scoured through this to remove all items that require explanation for which you have none. By

the time you're finished mowing the lawn or doing the dishes, most of what is left of your be-
longings will be spotless. Kiss your mother on the
cheek. It will make her feel good. Appreciated.

17. Beg for Money

Even when you don't need any. This way your parents will know you still need them for something.

18. Call Home

Even if you don't have anything to say to them, call mom and dad when you know they're either asleep or not at home and just leave a message. Sometimes they just want to hear the sound of your voice, to know that you're still alive and that they still matter to you.

19. Eat Your Vegetables

(and other food with some nutritional value)

They do wonderful things for your body that a Big Mac or Whopper, large fries and Krispy Kremes chased with a supersized Coke will never ever do. If this is difficult to achieve, take a really good grown-up multiple vitamin once a day or snack on dried prunes. They work. Besides: garbage in, garbage out!

20. Try to Get at Least Eight Hours of Sleep at Night, Not During the Day

Even though you're young, the body still needs sleep. Your brain is trying to get used to working harder than ever. Plus, you will not look like you're on one long hangover. And rest assured, you will probably go through the college rite of passage and have to pull an all-nighter to cram for Basket Weaving as It Relates to the Sociopolitical Milieu in the New Millennium 102A, so instead of relying on Red Bull or an extra-hot soy mocha macchiato with an extra five shots, try to get as many *Z*s as you can so you look and feel rested, which is not a bad thing.

21. Get Physical

Of course you hated P.E. in high school, but you *had* to sweat it out for four long years. Now you're free, but free to do what? Nothing? In college you don't have to take P.E., but try at least to get in some form of physical activity (and not you-know-what!) besides walking or riding your bicycle back and forth to class. Slam that tennis ball two or three times a week. Jog. Swim. Play volleyball. Basketball. Ballet. Pilates. Something. Anything to get your heart rate up and beating and have you going back to the dorm drenched in sweat! Your mind will appreciate it. Your stress level will drop. And you'll be in great shape—something many of you don't worry about now. But with no consistent physical activity, in five or

ten years, you could look in the mirror and think you're seeing double. It can happen. P.S.: your body talks. Remember, personal hygiene is important. Even though mom isn't standing outside monitoring you, bathe often, preferably daily. Use some form of deodorant so you don't stink. And brush your teeth at least twice a day. There are other parts of the body that are also best when fresh.

22. Get a Job During the Summer

We know you've worked hard all year hitting the books and you deserve a break, and now you think the living is going to be easy, but just like college, life isn't cheap or free, so welcome to the real world. Get a job. And try not to come home for the whole summer. You may not realize it, but things have changed since you've been gone. And even though your parents have missed you, there's a chance they've adjusted to your absence. In fact, don't be surprised if your old room is now a gym or if it's gone all together because mom and dad have moved into a condo at the beach!

23. If You Drink, Try Not to Get Sloppy Drunk, and if You Can, Avoid Doing Drugs

Let's face it, most college students booze it up, but if you just have to drink, know your limit. Many become binge drinkers. Some have ended up dead. They see getting smashed anytime they feel like it as a sign of independence and freedom and being grown up. But it's not. It's stupid. If you can't remember what you did or where you slept the night before, it's time to chill. If every time you drink you have to get disgustingly drunk, it's time to get a grip. Know your limit. And stick to it. Alcoholics can be bred in college. And how about this? If most adults got drunk every time they just felt like it or whenever they were a little stressed, many of you probably wouldn't even be here. The best way to appreciate life is to be present to feel it. Pain and discomfort are opportunities to grow—to see what you're made of. How you handle stress will reveal your true character and determine the quality of your life. Getting stoned is not even a temporary solution because when you come down everything is still where it was, maybe even worse. Now, it's just a suggestion, but try not to do any drugs if at all possible. Especially E and crank or crystal meth. Not one of them will help you do anything except get high. Besides, there are hundreds of healthy things you can do if you just need to chill out or want to escape and they have no side effects.

24. It Ain't Over 'Til the Fat Lady Sings!

It may be hard to imagine, but one day some of you will probably sit in a gymnasium or football field and watch *your* son or daughter march in a cap and gown and you'll probably cry and feel nostalgic because you'll remember the moment when you couldn't wait for all this graduation stuff to be over and done with so you could hurry up and get on down to Puerto Rico or Cancún or Maui and party your brains out and finally! finally! finally! be a grown-up! OK. So you'll party. And you'll come home and work a few short weeks at some menial job and then your bags will be all packed and mom and dad will drop you off at your college of choice (or not), and your first night in the dorm room you might

realize that you're not at sleep-away camp this time and this doesn't feel like your queen-sized bed at all and you sure wish you'd brought your Lovey or that Winnie-the-Pooh night-light, but hey, "It ain't no thang," so you'll just have to adjust to that twin bed and maybe one or two strangers commonly referred to as your roommates who now live in this miniature room with you called home, but if you feel a little bit nervous or scared or even lonely on this—your very first night at college—do what E.T. did: *phone home!*